Miles Prance

A True Narrative and Discovery

of several very remarkable passages relating to the horrid Popish plot

Miles Prance

A True Narrative and Discovery
of several very remarkable passages relating to the horrid Popish plot

ISBN/EAN: 9783337257071

Printed in Europe, USA, Canada, Australia, Japan

Cover: Foto ©ninafisch / pixelio.de

More available books at **www.hansebooks.com**

At the Court at VVhitehall
May 24. 1679.

In purſuance of His Majeſties Order in Council I Licenſe this Narrative to be printed.

SVNDERLAND.

By Virtue of this Order I appoint Dorman Newman Citizen and Stationer of London to print this Narrative.

May 26th 16 7 9.   *Miles Prance.*

Mr. Miles Prance.

Discoverer of the Horrid Plott
and the Murtherers of Sr. E. B Godfrey.

Printed for DORMAN NEWMAN at the Kings Armes in ye Poultrey.

A TRUE
NARRATIVE
AND
DISCOVERY

Of several very

REMARKABLE PASSAGES

Relating to the

𝕳𝖔𝖗𝖗𝖎𝖉 𝕻𝖔𝖕𝖎𝖘𝖍 𝕻𝖑𝖔𝖙:

As they fell within the Knowledge of

Mr *MILES PRANCE* of *Covent-Garden,*

GOLDSMITH.

VIZ.

I. His Depositions concerning the Plot in General
and a Particular Design against the Life of His
SACRED MAJESTY.

II. The whole Proceedings touching the Murther of
Sir *EDMUNDBURY GODFREY,*
and the particular Circumstances thereof.

III. A Conspiracy to murther the Right Honourable
the EARL of *Shaftsbury.*

IV. The Traiterous Intrigues and Immoralities of divers Popish Priests.

𝕻𝖚𝖇𝖑𝖎𝖘𝖍𝖊𝖉 𝖇𝖞 𝕬𝖚𝖙𝖍𝖔𝖗𝖎𝖙𝖞.

LONDON,

Printed for *Dorman Newman* at the Kings Arms in
the *Poultrey,* 1679.

THE
EPISTLE DEDICATORY
TO ALL
PROTESTANTS.

I Lookt upon the following Narrative as justly due to the World, whether I respected my Self or You: for as I am bound to disburden my own Conscience by a full and Impartial Discovery of what I know, relating to this horrid, detestable Popish Plot, and to endeavour to render my Acknowledgements as publick as the Evils wherein I have been involv'd; So I am under the Obligations of Charity to Contribute All I can to your Information and Satisfaction, That both the present Age, and Posterity may take right measures of Popery, as a thing so destructive to Government and Humane Society in general, and so directly opposite to all the Ennobling, Holy, Humble, Meek and Peaceable Designs of True Christianity, That the Better Roman-Catholick any person is, the worse man he becomes, and look how much more devout, so much the more dangerous.

For as when the Philistins had once deprived Sampson of his sight, they made him grinde in their Mill at their pleasure; so when people shut their Eyes, and give up themselves to be led blindfold by the Nose with a strong conceit, That they are Embarked in a Church that cannot Err, (which is the very Corner stone of the Romish Building, and the first Principle they infuse; although in truth, by that Church is meant nothing more than the Usurping, Domineering Pope, and his Covetous, Juggling, Self-designing Clergys;) After, I say, they are brought into this slavish hoodwinkt condition, 'tis no wonder, if they be led forwards by the same men, to the most wicked Practices, as well as false Opinions. For as the Understanding is directed, so the man, if he have any thing of a zealous temper, or be firm to the Religion he professes, will suitably Act, and consequently may with ease be seduced to think he does God the best service, when indeed he most violates all Laws of God, Nature and Man.

This I may the more firmly avouch, because I must acknowledge my self to have been an unhappy Example of it, and therefore although these abominable Principles and Practices of the Roman Church are already excellently laid open by a multitude of Learned men, (for She has bestow'd too many sad instances thereof on the World, and this Nation in particular,) Yet what I have to say, being matter of Fact, so lately done, and whereon I my self was so nearly concern'd, it may (though never so meanly delivered,)

A

The Epistle Dedicatory

delivered,) possibly with some be of use, more effectually to prevail with them.

The matters herein discovered are of a various, but all of them of a most black and villainous nature; some relate to the Plot in general, wherein you may perceive how far the design was spread, and how no small Number (to my knowledge) were privy thereunto, and certainly the poison must be most virulent at the Root when so many little Twiggs were therewith infected. You will find here (besides what hath been already discovered and proved by others) notice of a cursed hand that durst resolve to attempt the Sacred Life of our most Gracious Soveraign; a Prince, who besides the awful stamp of Heaven in His Character and Dignity, and the dread Life-guard of Sacred Precepts, Not to touch the Lords Anointed, carries in His Person such charms of Sweetness, Goodness, Clemency and Indulgence, as might secure him from violence even amongst Heathens and Savages; but no Quality or Innocence is Armour of proof against a Popish Knife; no Virtue sufficient to guard any from the Assassinations of a thorow-pac'd Jesuited Roman-Catholick.

And certainly the Murther of that Loyal Protestant-Magistrate, Sir Edmundbury Godfrey, was a thing so hellish in it self, and yet through Gods Over-ruling Providence, so very considerable in its influences to this poor Nations preservation, That I am confident it will be no mean satisfaction to all good Protestants to be ascertained of all (even the smallest) Circumstances relating thereunto; which as far as came within my knowledge, I have here freely and faithfully set forth, without adding a word beyond the Truth, out of prejudice, or any sinister end; or concealing any thing for my own Reputation; For though to commit Sin be the greatest of shame, yet ingenuously and penitently to confess it, to the Glory of God, and warning of our Neighbour, is no disgrace, but the greatest Honour, and the best service a seduced Criminal can be capable of, or able to perform.

Nor was their other Conspiracy against the Life of that Noble Lord, the Right Honourable the Earl of Shaftsbury herein likewise set forth, less wicked and barbarous on their part in the design, though frustrated by the Providence of God, who I trust will continually bring to nought all the mischievous Counsels of these Romish Achitophels, and cast the cruel Devices of such Assassinates on their own heads.

As for that part which concerns the Ill Lives of several of their Priests, the same is not inserted out of any Spleen or Ill will to their Persons, (for to several of them in the Course of my Trade I have been beholden, as far as they were my Customers) but to give our English World a Taste of the practises of the Leading men of that Apostate Church, and to perswade, if possible, Lay-Romanists, to consider what

kind

kind of *Perſons they are,* **on** *whoſe Sleeves they ſo blindly* pin their Faith, *and to whoſe Conduct they Truſt in a matter of ſuch unſpeakable Importance, as the Salvation or Eternal Deſtruction of their Souls. And this I the rather Recommend, and hope may be prevalent with* others, *becauſe it had ſome Weight with my ſelf; for next to Reflections on the odious* Plot *they were Carrying on, and the vile Murther* **they** *had Engaged me in,* The certain knowledge of the cloſe Hypocriſie or groſs Prophaneſs and lewd Lives *of their Ghoſtly Fathers (at leaſt moſt of thoſe I had the unhappineſs to be intimately Acquainted with, which were not a few, though I accuſe not All in that particular) had a ſtrong Influence to awaken my Thoughts to quit their Communion; As conceiving that muſt be a bad Cauſe which us'd ſuch wicked Means to ſupport it, and that it was no way likely* That *ſhould be the true Religion, which had no better Influence on the Converſations of thoſe who were its* Prieſts *and chief Promoters.*

The *far greateſt* part of this *whole Narrative* hath *already* been Atteſted upon Oath: *As for the reſt that is therein aſſerted, as on my own knowledge, I ſhall at any time be ready to Juſtifie and prove the ſame: And what I received by Information from others, is* every *where ſo Expreſſed, with the Reaſons and Circumſtances inducing the Credit I gave thereunto. For as I was Educated amongſt them from my Childhood, ſo I had a great Acquaintance and Familiarity with many of the* Fathers *and moſt zealous perſons of that party about the Town, having been ſeveral years her Majeſties Goldſmith, and the chief of my Trade depending on Prieſts and others of the Roman Catholick Perſwaſion.*

The reaſon why I preſume to Dedicate this mean Narrative to ſo great a Body as all You *worthy Proteſtants in General, ſeemeth to me* juſt, *becauſe* ſincere, *and* excuſable, *becauſe in ſome ſort* neceſſary; *I make you as it were All parties to theſe Preſents, not only that there may be ſo many* Living Witneſſes againſt me, *if ever either there ſhould be any wilful untruth found therein, Or that I ſhould fall back, (which God forbid) from that pure Religion which you profeſs, and I moſt cordially though lately have Embraced; But alſo more eſpecially thereby to Engage your* united Prayers *to God, as well for my* Perſeverance *and growth in Chriſtian Knowledge, as for my* Preſervation *againſt the Malice of thoſe reſtleſs Enemies, from whom I am to expect the* worſt *that* Raging Revenge *can ſuggeſt, or cruel* Malice *Execute; partly for my Relinquiſhment of them, but much more for diſcloſing ſome of their Proceedings; Wherein already they have not been wanting, for beſides Lies and Slanders induſtriouſly ſpread, to vilifie and make me odious, and the depriving me (as far as in them lies) of the Means of a Livelihood, I was of late credibly informed of a reſolved Deſign againſt my*

Life,

Life, and that three perſons had dogged me for ſome time for that pur-
poſe: But the Lord is my God, of whom then ſhall I be
afraid: To his infinite Protection I reſign my ſelf, and next under
him to that of his Vicegerent, from whoſe moſt gracious Majeſty,
as likewiſe from the Noble Lords of his moſt Honourable Counel, as well
as the Right Honourable the Houſe of Peers, I have upon all occaſions
found all juſt Encouragement, and very great Indulgence, which with
a thankful heart I deſire to commemorate, and publiſh for the Encourage-
ment of others.

The Romaniſts (eſpecially the Jeſuits and Prieſts, who ſway the
reſt at their pleaſure) are a moſt vigilant and unwearied ſort of People
to propagate their falſe Doctrines, and ſpread their Tyranny; I ſpeak
it Experimentally, who have had the advantage in a great meaſure to
know them; no Defeat can daunt them, nor ſcarce any Diſappoint-
ments diſcourage them: no ſooner is one Plot diſcovered, but they
preſently lay another. For 'tis a Rule that their Prieſts injoyn their
people to believe, I may I am confident ſay of moſt, as firmly as their
Creed, That their Religion ſhall infallibly one day or other be reſto-
red and eſtabliſhed again in England; and being thus verily perſwa-
ded, they *bear up under all Miſcarriages, and ſtill vigorouſly purſue*
the *main deſign, though in New Methods, and with different In-*
ſtruments. And therefore it will certainly concern Proteſtants to be as
careful and Active to prevent their Deſigns, and preſerve their own Re-
ligion and Lives, as the other are to deſtroy Both: you have now an Op-
portunity put into your hands to cruſh the Cockatrices Egge: O may you
all in your ſeveral places and ſtations improve it with Wiſdom, and with
Courage, and with Integrity: For if the Neck of their Deſign be not now
throughly broken, if Popery be not now Ham-ſtring in England; If
the Serpents Head be not bruiz'd, and the Vitals deſtroyed, it may juſtly
be feared, that it **will Revive** *again, and then the Plot will be only laid to*
ſleep, and not prevented, and the latter end prove worſe than the beginning.

But who am I, to adviſe ſo great and ſo wiſe a Body? May the God
of Wiſdom adviſe you and direct you, and protect you in his Truth and
in his Fear. And ſo begging all your Prayers on my behalf, I ſhall con-
clude, and ſubſcribe my ſelf

Covent-Garden.
May 26. 1679.

A Hearty Well-wiſher to the Proteſtant
Church, and the Welfare of the
King and People,

Miles Prance.

A NARRATIVE

OF

The whole PROCEEDINGS touching the

MURTHER

OF

Sir *EDMUND-BURY GODFREY*;

AND

Several other Paſſages relating to the

Horrid Popiſh Plot,

Which came within the Knowledge of

MILES PRANCE,

Of St. *Giles's in the Fields*, in the County of *Middleſex*,

GOLDSMITH.

MIles *Prance* was from his Infancy bred up in that Perſwaſion, which calls it ſelf the Roman Catholick Religion, having ſeveral very near Relations engaged therein; and being under the ſtrong Prejudices of Education, and continual Incitements of the Prieſts, was very zealous for advancing that Church ; being made believe, That in order to that end, no means ought to be avoided or eſteemed unlawful.

B   He

He had, by long Conversation, contracted as large and intimate an Acquaintance both with the Priests and Jesuits residing in *England*, (especially about *London*) as also with Persons of Quality of the Romish Profession, as any man of his Circumstances was capable of.

He doth well know, that for divers years last past, it hath been a General Opinion and Expectation amongst Papists, That their Religion should in some short time be publickly Re-established in *England*. And this vain Conceit their Priests did always very industriously nourish in them, but with words more open and peremptory here of late, than before: so that he, as well as others, had for several years, a general Intimation, That some great thing was shortly to be done for the Roman Catholick Cause, and that the Redemption (as they were wont to call it) was drawing nigh. But the first direct and particular Information he received of the Plot, or any formed Design and Resolution to take Arms, was near two years ago, on the occasion, and in the manner following, *viz.*

One Mr. *Towneley* of *Towneley* in *Lancashire*, a Gentleman of a very considerable Estate, coming up to *London* with his two Sons, in order to carrying them over to *Doway*, there to be brought up : For that is the general practice of the Popish Gentry, to send over their Children thither, being made believe, that we have no good method of Learning in our English Schools or Universities : but that the only grand Masters of Education in the World, are the Jesuits. By which means, not only our Nation is scandaliz'd, and the Wealth thereof privately drain'd away, but also it comes to pass, that the Children of so many Noble and Considerable Families, being bred up from their tender years wholly under their Tuition, they have the better opportunities to instil Traiterous and Disloyal Principles into their minds, plant in them an endless hatred against the Protestant Religion, and in general, gain such an Ascendant over them, that as they were their Masters and Tutors in their Youth, so they behave themselves as their Governours all their lives afterwards : the Estates of many Popish Gentry being as absolutely at the Priests dispose, as at their own.

own. These things he knows to be true, and of very pernicious Consequence ; and therefore hopes 'tis no unseasonable digression to mention them.

This Mr. *Townley* coming to Town on this occasion, did likewise bring up with him his two Brothers to keep him Company, and took Lodgings at one *Aries* house in *Drury-Lane*, where *John Fenwick*, a notorious Jesuite and Arch-traitor, now in custody, then had his Residence : where, after they had continued some short time, the said Mr. *Townley* and one of his Brothers went over to *Doway* with the two Lads, and left the other here ; who, in the absence of his Brothers, declared very often to Mr. *Prance's* Wives Brother, and to one *Adamson* a Watch-maker, That when his Brothers came back from *Flanders*, they expected to receive Commissions from the Lord *Bellasis* and other Catholick Lords concern'd, for the raising of men to carry on the Catholick Cause. And this his Brother and the said *Adamson* several times told again to Mr. *Prance* at *Pedley's* house in *Vere-street*, where was kept a frequent Club, consisting of none but Papists.

That during the time that the Duke of *Buckingham*, the Earl of *Shaftsbury*, the Lord *Wharton* , and Lord *Salisbury*, were confined in the Tower, one Mr. *Keighly*, a person (reputed) of good Estate, was pleased in discourse to express his joy and satisfaction for such their Confinement : For, said he, *Now is the time for the Promoting of Catholick Religion* ; (meaning Popery ;) *and if his Royal Highness be but sure, and will follow the Business closely*, (which he said Catholicks had good grounds to hope he would) *and we can but strike whilst the Iron is hot, and not lose opportunities, I do not doubt but our Religion may speedily be settled in* England · *for no juncture of time can appear more fair or favourable for the Business than the present.*

That about a year ago, being in Company with one *Singleton* a Popish Priest, at the house of one *Hall* a Cook in *Ivy-lane, London*, the said Priest, in the presence of Mr. *Prance* and the said *Hall*, did say these Words following : *That he hoped he should be settled in a Parish Church before a Twelvemonth came about ; for he did not fear but that the Catholick Re-*
ligion

ligion would reign in England: *and to advance it*, *he would not make any more matter to Stab Forty Parliament-men, than to eat his Dinner* he being then sitting at Dinner with his Knife in his hand. Concerning this zealous Gentlemans pranks, we shall have occasion to speak more hereafter.

That one Mr. *Ridley* a Chirurgion, living at the House that was late the Lord *Baltimore's* in *Wild-street*, walking in *Wild-*Garden, declared, That he expected to be a Chirurgion to the Catholick Army in *England*; and that he hoped the Lord *Bellasis*, whom he knew was one chief person to Command it, would much stand his friend in that concern. And since the Discovery of the Plot, upon Mr. *Prance's* information, there was a Popish Priest, one *Fincham* by name, being a Priest to the Lady *Savel*, taken in the said Mr. *Ridley's* House, where he was sheltered: but since, by the mediation of good friends, he is, as 'tis said, sent beyond the Seas.

That in the Month of *August*, 1678. Mr. *Prance* having occasion to write to a friend in the Countrey, but not knowing certainly how to send, went to one Mr. *Paston*, whom he had some reasons to believe could inform him therein; he lodged then at one *Bamber's* a Taylor in *Duke-street*, and had great resort of Jesuits and Priests to his Chamber: after he had satisfied him in the particular matter he came to him about, they immediately fell into discourse of publick Affairs, and the interest of Catholick Religion; and he bid Mr. *Prance* not to fear any thing, for all would suddenly be well: for in the first place, he said, *It was true, the King was a great Heretick, but the Lord* Bellasis, *the Lord* Arundel, *the Lord* Powis, *and Lord* Peters, (these four Noblemen he well remembers he named) *would have a gallant Army for the Deposing, or Disposing* (he cannot now certainly say which of those words he used, but is sure it was one of them) *of the King, and utter subversion of all the Protestants; and then the Catholick Religion should be establish'd and flourish in this Nation.* And he then further said, *That the Lords had already given out Commissions to divers Gentlemen in the Country for raising their Troops;* and he named several of them; amongst whom he well remembers one was Mr. *Talbot* of *Longford*; another, Sir *Henry Bedingfield* of *Ox-*

borough

borough-hall in *Norfolk*, and a third Mr. *Stone*, who lives within four or five miles of *Kingston* upon *Thames*: others he mentioned, whose names he does not so well retain.

7. That about eight or ten days before *Michaelmass*, 1678. he had a more clear discovery of the Design in hand, That they intended to leavy War, to subvert the Government, &c. for being at the Chamber of Father *Ireland* the Jesuite, since Executed for Treason, he lodging then in *Russel-street*, where were likewise present *John Fenwick* and *John Grove*; the said *Ireland* did declare, *That they would VERY SHORTLY be Fifty thousand men in Arms.* At which Mr. *Prance*, as surprised, demanded of him, where they would have them, and what they were to do? to which he answered, *We must have them speedily to settle our Religion here, or else all will be ruined.* Then Mr. *Prance* inquired who should command them? to which *Fenwick* undertook to make answer, and said, *That they should be Commanded by the Lord* Arundel, Lord Bellasis, Lord Powis, *and others.* Whereupon, Mr. *Prance* apprehending the fatal mischiefs and distractions of a Civil War, said to them, *What then shall we poor Tradesmen do?* the same *Fenwick* replyed, *You for your part of all men need not fear a Trade, for you* (being a Goldsmith) *will have enough in your way by Church-work.* And several such discourses then passed between them, whereby he plainly understood, that there was a grand Plot, and near to be put in execution, and that they were very confident of the success.

8. That soon after this, the said *Grove* came to Mr. *Prance's* shop to buy two Silver-spoons for a Christening where he was to be Godfather; and taking occasion to speak of their last recited discourse at Father *Ireland's*, Mr. *Prance* askt him what Office he the said *Grove* was to have in the Catholick Army: but he declined to answer directly, and at last said, *He did not know AS YET.* Then being askt again, who were to govern this intended Army, he named the Lord *Bellasis*, the Lord *Arundel*, the Lord *Powis*, and the Lord *Peters*; and said, that they had already Commissions for that purpose.

9. The Priests themselves were not only the grand Contrivers of this desperate Design, with Counsel and Encouragement,

C

ragement, but likewise intended to be actually concern'd in the Butcheries, as well as the Laiety : for very near the same time, Mr. *le Fevre* a Priest, whom Mr. *Prance* was well acquainted with, as having sold him several Chalices, Crewets, Basons, Oil-boxes for Extreme Unction, and such like Utensils, came to his Shop to buy a second-hand Silver-hilt for a Sword; whereupon, he askt him what he meant to do therewith, for he had a good Sword already ? The said *le Fevre* answered, there were times coming on, wherein Catholicks would have good occasion for Weapons, and therefore he would be sure to be provided, by getting another special Sword, and would have such an Hilt to it.

10. Happening one day to see Mr. *Moor*, that belongs to the Duke of *Norfolk*, riding in the streets upon a very brave Horse, meeting him soon after in the Court at *Somerset*-House, Mr. *Prance* was saying what a gallant Beast he saw him mounted upon lately : whereupon, the said Mr. *Moor* wished that he had ten Thousand of them ; but said, that he hoped in a very short time we should have Ten thousand as good Horses, and mounted with brave men, well Arm'd and Accoutred, for the advancing of the Catholick Cause : which he spoke openly, and in a braving manner, as if he were not afraid to own the thing, nor cared who heard him.

11. In like manner, and much about the same time, he heard Mr. *Messinger*, Gentleman of the Horse to the Lord *Arundel*, boast, That he doubted not but to see the Catholick Religion flourish ere long throughout *England*, and Hereticks to be rooted out : for he hoped to see a gallant Army one of these days, to effect so glorious a work. The same man was afterwards engaged in the horrid Designs of Murthering the Kings Sacred Majesty, and also of the Right Honourable the Earl of *Shaftsbury*; of which a particular Account is herein afterwards given.

After God, by a Miracle of Mercy to these Nations, had been pleased to give some Discovery of the Plot, their insolence was little daunted, and their malice encreased; contriving new ways to destroy all that opposed them, and to involve us in Blood and Confusion.---For,

12. When the Order came forth for tendring the Oaths of
Alle-

Allegiance and Supremacy to all *Roman Catholicks*, one Mr. *Laurence*, an Apothecary in *Drury-lane*, came to Mr. *Prance's* House, to borrow a Book which had in it the forms of the said Oaths, seeming very much dissatisfied and offended about it; and after several Complaints, and Murmurings against Authority, did speak these words---*I wish with all my heart, half the Parliament were poysoned*, *for they will ruine us all*, meaning all Papists. Now how exceeding dangerous may a person, continuing under such desperate Principles, and of that Trade, be to the Nation, in destroying privately, such as shall oppose their Hellish Design? for 'tis reasonably to be feared, that he that had mad zeal and malice enough to wish half the Members of that most Honourable Assembly poysoned, will scarce stick to try a piece of his skill upon any particular Heretick or Hereticks, when the Interest of their Bloody Church shall command, or prospect of considerable gain invite thereunto.

13. That about a fortnight before St. *Thomas's* day last, Mr. *Prance* having an intimate Acquaintance with the Lord *Arundel* of *Warder's* Butler, he told Mr. *Prance*, (but with a great obligation of Secrecy,) That the before-mentioned Mr. *Messinger* (his Lords Gentleman of the Horse) was to Kill the King, and to have a vast Reward, if he escaped with his Life, as 'twas well hoped, the business was so neatly contrived, that he might: But however, if he should miscarry or suffer in or for the Attempt, then he having appointed before-hand what Friends should have the said Reward, it should be distributed faithfully to them by the said Lord *Arundel*, *Powis*, and the rest of the Lords that were in the Plot. Whereupon, within a day or two after, *Prance* meeting with the said *Messinger* in *Lincolns-Inn-fields*, after some previous and preparatory discourse, asked him, *Why he would kill the King?* At which question he appeared strangely surprized and confounded, as wondering how he should come to know of such his Traiterous Intention: But Mr. *Prance* seeming not willing to give him any occasion of fear, he, recollecting himself, said, *Who told you of it?* To which the other answered, That their Butler intimated so much to him, as a Friend; whereupon he only said, No, no, we are off of
that

that thing now? giving him to understand as if they had taken some new Measures. Then Mr. *Prance* took leave of him, who seemed much troubled at the Discovery: and after he was gone a few paces from him, call'd him back again, and ask'd him to drink with him; but he told him, that his business required haste, and so avoided going with him. Then he adjur'd him not to speak of that business to any body living. But afterwards the poor Butler came to *Prance's* shop, and told him, That he had received great Anger, and was like to be undone, because he had told him what Mr. *Messinger* was to have done.

14. In the same street where Mr. *Prance* lives, *viz. Princes-street* in *Covent-Garden*, there dwells one *GROVE* a Papist, (Nephew to *John Grove*, lately executed for designing to murther the King) who is still, at the writing hereof, suffered to teach School there. This person, after the Condemnation of his Uncle, said very confidently, That there was no such Plot at all as was pretended, for it was only a Plot of the Protestants: And to vilifie the Kings Evidence, though most plain and pregnant, (according to the usual method of all Papists, who make it their grand business to throw upon them all imaginable Scandals) said, That they were all Rogues that swore against his Uncle. Whereupon Mr. *Prance* (of whom he then had no mistrust, but lookt upon him as firm to their Party) said, But then what think you of the Fifty thousand men that were suddenly to be raised? which to my knowledge he knew of: for I well remember he told me of it. Which plain Argument of his Uncles Treason from Mr. *Prance*, the said *Grove* not being able to deny, said, *That possibly his Uncle might speak that in jest.* Such sorry Evasions will they make use of to out-face Truth, bolster up their villainous Practices, and make ignorant and credulous people believe, That all their Traitors are Saints, or at least Martyrs.

Further Particulars which have fallen within the said *Miles Prance's* Cognizance touching the Plot in general, (though several material ones there are) we shall not here mention, as being not yet fit to be publickly divulg'd; but proceed to the Murther of Sir *Edmundbury Godfrey*, in which Mr. *Prance* was unhappily concern'd.

THE

THE FULL

DISCOVERY

OF THE

Manner and Circumstances

OF

Sir EDMUNBURY GODFREY's

MURTHER.

1. THe Design of Murthering this Innocent and Never-to-be-forgotten Gentleman was laid, and some Attempts made to Execute it before it was at all Communicated unto Mr. *Prance*, for he hath since heard by *Girald* and *Kelly* (Irish Popish Priests concerned in the Murther) and others, that once, some small time before they acquainted him with it ; a Gentleman passing by *Sommerset-House*, that was very like Sir *Edmondbury* in Stature, Physiognomy and Habit ; some of them mistook, and Complemented him as Sir *Edmondbury*, but the Stranger denying the Name, or that he was any such Person, they were so confident, as to think he did it out of Caution, to avoid them. And therefore peremptorily told him he was Sir *Edmonbury Godfrey*, which he as positively denying, they made some attempts to push him into the House, but at last perceiving their mistake, Released him, pretending it was only to have drank a Bottle of Wine with him. Likewise they said, that once or oftner, they had dogged him into the Fields, and out parts of the Town, but being in the day time, could meet with no opportunity to dispatch him.

2. On *Sunday*, wanting but a Day of a Fortnight before the Murther committed, coming from the Queen's Chappel, the said *Girald* and *Kelly*, together with *Robert Green*, Cushion-man to the Chappel, *Laurence Hill*, Doctor *Goddin's* Man (which Doctor is Treasurer of the Chappel) and Mr. *Prance* went (as commonly they did every Sunday) to the Plough-Alehouse by the *Watergate* (as they call it, that is the furthermost Gate or Passage going down out of the *Strand* to the Waterside) of *Sommerset-House* ; Where after some common friendly Discourse and Talk of the Plot

D   which

which was then begun to be discovered. *Girald* the Priest, in a familiar plausible way askt *Prance* if he did not know Sr. *Edmundbury Godfrey*, who told him he had heard of him, and seen him; but had no particular Acquaintance with him. Then he askt if he did not know what a bitter Persecutor he was to Catholicks, and a particular Enemy to the Queens Servants (which 'tis supposed he urged because *Prance* was one of them :) And now of late (said he) he has examined People against us, and got Depositions to fix odious Crimes and Scandals upon us and our Religion ; To which *Prance* answered that he heard he had lately taken some Examinations concerning the Plot, but did not know the particulars, though he understood there was a great deal of Noise abroad about it, and heard that Mr. *Ireland* and others last Night were taken upon it. The other told him that the said Sr.*Edmundbury* was so desperate an Enemy, and had done such things that if he were not taken off, the Catholicks would be generally ruined, and therefore it was absolutely necessary for the Glory of God, and the good of the Church that it be done. And if we can find an Opportunity to do it, we shall have a very good Reward from no worse Man than the Lord *Bellasis*, and therefore (saith the said *Girald* to *Prance*) looking upon you as a good Catholick and that will not deny so good a Service to the Church ; we would have you be aiding and assisting to us in it. This was the very Effect, and as neer as he can remember the Words of his first Discourse.

To which, being surprised with Horror at so unexpected and Cruel a Motion, *Prance* answered, no, he could not be concerned, nor would be Guilty of any Mans Blood for a World. For Murther was a greivous and most mortal Sin. The Priest replied, Alas, this is no Sin, but a Work of Charity. There is no Murther in this Case, it is for the Glory of God and the good of the Church, and therefore you ought to do it. With several other Words to that Purpose.

In which wicked Persuasions, *Kelly* the other Priest likewise joyned with him, affirming the same, and highly encouraging *Prance* and the rest present (whom it seems they had Engaged before) thereunto, as a meritorious Work. Yet still *Prance* told them he could not treacherously kill any Man, for he was not able to force his Mind to such an Action; *Girald* said, he desired him to be no further concerned than he would be himself, and that he would make nothing of killing twenty Hereticks in such a Case, and that there was no Danger in it, for it might easily be effected and no body the Wiser. Several such Words and Discourses passed.

sed. At last they told him he should not be troubled to do the
Business, but should only stand at a distance, and *that* they were
sure he would not deny to do, for, by their very declaring the Business, he was already as far concerned as that came to, unless he
would betray them, which if he did, he was certainely Damned,
nor should escape long here without Revenge.

These to the best of his Memory were the substance of all their
Arguments to him. Nor did they assign any particular reason of
their Malice, only that Sr. *Edmundbury Godfry* was a busy Man, and
was going about to ruine all the Catholicks in *England*, and that
it was necessary to destroy him, else they should be all undone. In
fine, so importunate they were, that by these cursed Persuasions
proceeding from Priests whom he had been taught to Reverence,
and receive their Words as Oracles; *Prance* was prevailed with,
(with hearty Sorrow, Shame and Contrition, he desires to acknowledg it) to keep their bloody Councels, not daring both on a Religious and Temporal Account to reveal the same, fearing as well
Damnation in the next World, if he should discover it, as Ruine
in this, being one of her Majesties Servants, and so great a part or
rather his whole Livelyhood depending on her and other Catholicks. With whom these revengful Priests by their Interest and
some false Informations might easily undo him, besides the Danger
he lay under of a private Stab or the like Mischief from them.

Then they acquainted him that some others were engaged in the
Business, besides those then present, naming *Henry Berry* Porter to
the Queens Majesty at the upper Court Gate, one *Lewson* a Priest,
and *Philip Vernatti*, who did belong to the Lord *Bellasis*, heretofore
Pay-master at *Tangier*, and much indebted to the said Lord. Who
together with *Gerrard* and *Kelly* (as tis believed) were the first
that were ingaged in the Business, and that the said *Vernatti* might
be induced thereto by some Promise, That his Debt should be
remitted, and further Rewards promised.

They likewise said there should be one more in it, whose Name
(as they then told it) he doth not remember. And as he since understands, there were several others concerned. So desperately were
the Original Contrivers set upon this good Gentlemans Murther;
That to effect it throughly they laid several distinct Plots, and Imployed diverse Seperate Agents unknown to each other. But those
above mentioned were all that he then knew of for his part, or
that they discovered to him.

3. In the Week following, some of them met with him several
times at the same House, and appointed to meet the next Sunday,
which accordingly they did: Walking *immediately from Prayers* at
the

the Chappel down to the Water-side, where they presently fell into Consultation about the manner of effecting this Horrid Murther. But did not there come to any Resolution, but went from thence to the said *Plough* to drink, where they concluded to dog or watch Sir *Edmundbury* the next Week, and that whoever of them could first see him in a Convenient Place, should give the rest notice.

4. Pursuant to this Resolve, as he since understood, *Green* and some of the rest were at Sir *Edmundbury's* House, and endeavoured to watch him, but as appears, could not light on a fit Opportunity. They met sometimes in the former part of that Week, but *Prance* never concerned himself to go to his House, or elsewhere, to look for, or after him; But on Saturday the twelfth of *October* in the Morning, *Girald*, *Green* and *Hill*, went forth to observe his Motions, and *Kelly* the other Priest who lodged in *Somerset-House*, and knew of their going, came about nine a Clock in the Forenoon to *Prance's* House, to acquaint him therewith, and charge him to be at home in a readiness; The first three went near Sir *Edmundbury Godfrey's*, and whilst two staid some little way off, *Hill* went up to his House, and enquired for Sir *Edmundbury*, and understanding he was within, Spake with him, and pretended some fained Business, as 'tis believed, but not certainly known what it was, and so he returned to his Companions. (This Account he relates as he had it from themselves, *viz. Girald* and *Green*, afterwards, being not present then himself, but at home as aforesaid.)

5. About ten or eleven a Clock Sir *Edmundbury* came forth all alone (as his manner was, for, being a Plain Stout Gentleman, he never or very seldom went abroad attended with any Servant, which they very well knew.) They waiting for him privately, dogged him to several Places, up and down all the rest of the Day, as his Business led him, till about six or seven a Clock at Night he came to S. *Clements*, and went into a great House there, where it is thought he supped. Then *Green* left the other two, and came to *Prance's* Shop, but he not being at home, but at a publick House hard by, he sent for him, and informed him, that they had now set Sir *Edmundbury* in S. *Clements* (but the particular House he did not name or declare to him, so as he might know whose it was) but only told him that he must make all the haste he could down to *Sommerset-House* to the Water-Gate, where he should find *Kelly* the Priest, and *Berry* the Porter; Accordingly *Prance* left his Company, went thither, and found them walking in the Yard, where they
three

three sometimes walking, and sometimes sitting on the Bench,
continued till about nine of the Clock; And then Sr. *Edmundbury* as it appears came forth of the said Place by St. *Clements,*
and presently *Hill* came runing away before, up Street to give
Notice that he was coming. And ordered that for to wheadle him
in, two should pretend to be a Quarrelling, and having thus said,
the said *Hill* goes up again to the Water-Gate, and stood there
to expect his coming by, and intice him in. In the mean time
Kelly the Priest and *Berry* began a seeming Quarrel, but made no
great Noise; and Sr. *Edmundbury* coming along the *Strand*, just
as he was passing by the Water-Gate, *Hill* (who well knew
Sr. *Edmundbury,* and Sr. *Edmundbury* him, as having traded with
him for Coals) steps up to him as in a great deal of Haste, and
says, for God sake, Sr. *Edmundbury Godfrey* be pleased to come
in, for here are two Men a Quarrelling, and I am afraid there
will be Blood shed between them. Pough, Pough, said Sr.
Edmundbury, refusing at first to trouble himself, but *Hill* still cry-
ing out he feared there might be a great deal of Harm done, and
how glad he was to light on his Worship, who being a Magistrate,
his Presence would presently quiet them, and therefore intreated
him again just to step in; The Gallant Gentlemans good Nature, was such, not suspecting any Harm, but designing to do
an Act of Charity, and to endeavour that the Peace might be
kept according to his Office, that he was prevailed with by
the Treacherous Persuasions of the Assassinate, to turn into the
Trap they had laid for him.

6. *Hill* entred the Gate first, Sr. *Edmundbury* follows him
and immediately behind him, *Girald* and *Green*; they coming
down as soon as they had past *Prance* (who stood close up to
the Wall unseen) went forwards towards the Water-Gate, to observe any that should come that way, and *Bury* then went
to secure the Stairs and Passage by the Chappel. But first he
and *Kelly* were the pretended Quarrellers, and stood just at
the end of the Raile by the Queens Stables, and as Sr. *Edmundbury* went down, *Green* who walkt just behind him, having in
readiness a large twisted Handkerchif, on a sudden threw the
same about his Neck, and immediately they all sower, viz. *Girald, Kelly, Green* and the said *Hill* fell upon him, secured his
Sword, pull'd him down, throtled him, so that he could nei-
ther Cry out, nor Speak, drew him behind the Rail and
gave him many violent Punches on the Breast with their
Knees, and having as they supposed dispatcht him, and that he had
lain still for a while, fearing he was not yet quite dead, *Girald* the Priest would have run his Sword through him, but the

E   rest

rest would not yield to that, for they said then it would be discovered by the Blood, so that at their Persuasion he put up his
Sword again, and did not do it; however to make sure work,
Green got upon him, and punching him with all his Force on the
Breast with his Knee, wrung his Neck round; The first Attack,
viz. Green's flinging the twisted Handkerchief about his Neck,
and their falling upon him, *Prance* saw, and then immediately
went to the Water-Gate, and as for the rest of the Transactions,
he had it from all their Mouths afterwards, and particularly as to
the wringing of his Neck, *Green* told of it himself, for he boast-
ed of it; and the bloody minded Priest *Girald*, seeing him Dead,
said these Words: *Well, if we could not have enticed him in here, I
resolved I would have followed him down* Hartf-horn Lane *that leads
to his own House, and there would have run him through with my own
Hand.*

But it was otherwise ordered by the Hand of God, who
though he sometimes suffers wicked Men to perpetrate their
barbarous Designs, yet he often over-rules them so far as that
they themselves against their Intentions, contribute to the Discovery, or brings by infinite Wisdom and Power, Good out of
Evil, and serves the Interests of his Church and People even
by the Cruelty of their implacable Enemies. For had they
killed him in another Place, or disposed of his Body in another
manner, 'tis possible it had never been found out, and in that
Case, or if they had not been suffered to be so far infatuated
by the Devil as to Murther him; 'tis probable their Hellish Plot
had never been sufficiently taken notice of, till felt in the direful
Effects, so that Sir *Edmundbury* must justly be stiled, *The King and
Kingdoms Martyr*, since his Death (though in it self most horrid
and deplorable) was yet through the infinite Mercy of God, a
means to preserve the Lives of many Thousands.

7. Having staid at the Gate about a Quarter of an Hour,
in all which time no body offered to come in that way, *Prance*
went down to them, and likewise *Berry* came from his Post at
the Stairs, and then they all set upon removing the Body,
which they carried in at a Door right against the place where
he was Murthered, and so up a Pair of Stairs that goes into a
long Entry leading into the upper Court by the Coach-Houses,
and then into Doctor *Godlin's* Lodgings, who was Treasurer of the
Chappel to the Queen, where the said *Hill* lived, and did all the
Doctor's Business, being the first Door on the left Hand in the
said Entry, *Hill* going before and opening the Door; Then they
carried him up five or six Steps, into a little Room on the Right
Hand, where they set the Body with his Back leaning against a
Bed,

Bed, and so leaving *Hill* there as being at home, the rest departed, and dispersed themselves, every Man to his own Dwelling; getting home about ten of the Clock, or between ten and eleven.

8. The Body lay in that Room, Saturday-Night, Sunday all Day and Night, and until Munday at Night, and then *Prance* coming from Home about ten of the Clock down to *Hill's* to know if they had disposed thereof, or how they would do it, because he had heard nothing from them; *Hill* told him, that he and the rest had that Evening a little before, carried him out to a Room cross the upper Court of *Sommerset-House*, for fear Notice should be taken of their keeping the other Room so long private, or that some Body should have occasion to go into it, and discover him; then Mr. *Prance* went to the *Plough Ale-House*, where he found *Green*, *Girald* and *Kelly*, and presently *Hill* came thither also, and *Hill* with a Dark Lanthorn went with the other three, &c. to shew Mr. *Prance* where the Body lay, which was in the said Room in the upper Court upon the Ground, covered with a Cloth over the Head, but his Sword was not there, but still kept hidden in *Hill's* House; So having seen the Body, every Man went home.

9. There the Corps continued Munday-Night, and all Tuesday till about nine of the Clock at Night, and then all the said five Persons, *viz. Girald*, *Kelly*, *Green*, *Hill* and *Berry* took him out of the said Room, and brought him back cross the Court-Yard to the aforesaid long Entry by Doctor *Goddin's* Door, but *Hill* going in before to his own Lodging, found (as they declared after) some Body there, so that they could not with safety lay him in the same Room where he was first before, and therefore they carried him into another Room on the left Hand going from the upper Court just opposite to Doctor *Goddin's* Door, which, as is supposed, was Sir *John Arunde's* Lodgings, who is Master of the Horse to the Queen.

10. There the Body lay Tuesday-Night, and till Wednesday about nine a Clock at Night; and then all the said five persons undertook to convey it back again to the Room in Doctor *Goddin's* Lodgings where *Hill* lived, and where it was laid at first, they imagining, as Mr. *Prance* supposes, that they might have more freedom, and better opportunity to carry it from thence unperceived, than from the other place; but during the time they were so removing him, and just as they had the Body in the Entry, Mr. *Prance* accidentally came that way, and they not knowing who it might be, left the Body there, and began to fly, *Berry* running away quite to his Lodge, but Mr. *Prance* calling to them, they knowing his Voice, came back, and then they all (but *Berry* who was so gone) set to their Hands and got it up again into the said little Room in Doctor *Goddin's* Lodgings, where it was at first.

There

11. There they entred into a serious Consultation, and the two Priests *Girald* and *Kelly* (whether by order of Superiors or not, cannot here be set forth because they named no body that had so ordered, but delivered it as their own Sense) advised that the safest and best way was to carry him out into the Fields and lay him in some obscure Place, in such a manner as that when ever he should be found it might be supposed that he murther'd himself, which would much serve the Interest of the Church, when it should be publickly known, that he who was so busy in charging Catholicks with a Plot, was so troubled afterwards for so abusing them in the same, that he made away himself; and therefore it was agreed that none of his Mony or other things should be medled with, the better to colour that Report; and indeed if they did take away any Note-Book or other Writing from him, it was in *Prance's* absence, for he never saw them search his Pockets, nor doth know what became of his Band, but supposes the same might be lost in some of their removes, and being found by some Papist, when the Body was after discovered, and enquiry made after the Band, the same might be kept concealed, because it should not be any Evidence that he was murthered there.

12. This being well approved of, it was further resolved to carry the Body away that Night about twelve of the Clock, to which Purpose *Hill* and another undertook to get a Sedan, and appointed all to meet there at eleven a Clock; in the mean time they went home. Mr. *Prance* calling as he passed, upon *Berry* to let him know that he must be ready on such a Sign to open the Gate.

13. Near eleven a Clock that Night Mr. *Prance* returned, and found all the four; *viz. Hill, Green, Girald* and *Kelly* there, and a Sedan provided, standing ready at Doctor *Goddin's* Door. Now by that time they had contrived which way to carry him and got him into the Sedan, it was neer twelve a Clock, then *Gyrald* and *Prance* going to carry him, found there wanted Leathers and were not able to carry him well with their Arms, so *Hill* provided Cords, which they tyed in the nature of Leathers, and then *Gyrald* and *Prance* took him up and carried him over the Court-Yard up to the Lodge and there gave an Hum (which was the Token agreed on) and thereupon *Bury* came forth and opened the Gate and let them out, having on purpose to avoide any Notice being taken, invited the Souldiers into his House with Drink and Tobacco, for they saw no Centinel at all, and at the Tryal, the Souldiers which that Night stood Centinel acknowledged that they saw a Sedan come in, but none go out, and indeed it was Impossible they should, they not being there, but in *Bury's* House, where were Lights seen and Company heard talking.

Being

Being thus got out of *Sommerset*-House, *Hill* run before to
get ready an Horse. But whose the Horse was, and where provided, Mr. *Prance* doth not know. Then *Girald* and *Prance*
carried him into *Covent-Garden* to the end of St. *James's-street*, and
there set him down; and then *Kelly* and *Green*, who walkt by
took him up and carried him along *Kings-street* to *Newstreet*-
end, and so up *Rose-street* to *Long-acre-end*. Then the first two
took him again, and carried him by the *Grey-hound* Tavern
to the *Grecian* Church, there *Hill* met them with an Horse,
and taking out the Body, set it on the Horse before *Hill*, and
clapt the Sedan into an House that was building, but unfurnisht,
leaving it there till they came back. The Body being so set
on Horse-back, *Girald* the Priest said, *I wish we had an hundred
such Rogues as secure as we have this*. Then those four, viz.
Hill, Girald, Kelly and *Green*, went away with him, one leading the Horse, and the other walking by on each side, whilst
Hill held him on before him. But Mr. *Prance* returned home,
because being an House-keeper his Family might take no notice
of his being out all night, nor any body observe his coming
home in the Morning, for it was between One and before Two
he got back.

14. Next day they met together, and then *Girald* told him
that they had laid the Body in a Ditch belonging to a Field a-
bout *Primrose*-Hill; and to make people think whenever he shall
be found, That he kill'd himself, I, said he, run his own Sword
through him, and left it in his Body, and laid his Scabbard and
Gloves at a small distance on the Bank.

15. On the Thursday in the Afternoon the Body was
found: That night Mr. *Prance* was at the *Horseshoo*-Tavern
in *Drury*-Lane, with *Philip Veniatti*, that should have been
actually concern'd in the Murther, but fail'd to be there; and
also another friend that accidentally was with them, knowing
nothing in the least of this horrid business. There some people
came in and said, That Sir *Edmundbury Godfrey* was found murthered. Whereupon the said *Vernatti* calling Mr. *Prance* aside
to the Fire, said, Lord! is this mans Body found already that
was carried away but yesternight! Thanks be to God that he
was convey'd away without any notice, for now I hope it will never be discover'd. He said further, That he should have been
concern'd, and was sent to, but was not at home, but was sorry he
was not there, to have been assistant to them. Then he ask'd the
manner how the Murther was contrived; of which Mr. *Prance*

F   gave

gave him some short account, but not all, because his Friend being in the Room, they were afraid of talking long so privately,
lest he should suspect something to their prejudice.

16. In little time after, the said *Vernatti* met with *Girald*,
who gave him an exact Account in Writing of the whole
proceedings and manner of the Murther, That he (as he said)
might communicate and shew the same to the Lord *Bellasis*, and
other original Designers or promoters of the business, for their satisfaction; which Mr *Prance* came to the knowledge of in manner following, *viz.* About a fortnight afterwards he met with
the said *Vernatti* again, who invited him to *Bow* to take a Dinner, and see a Friend of his: To which he consented, and the
day was appointed. But in the morning they were first to meet
in *London* at the *George*, an Alehouse right over against the *Stocks*
Market; where going accordingly, he found Mr. *Vernatti* and
the before-mentioned *Lewson*, a Priest that was privy to the Murther, and should likewise have been at it, but happened to be
absent; these were got thither before, but Mr. *Prance* had but
a little time been come to them, before the said *Vernatti* pluckt
out of his Pocket a Paper in which was written down an account
of the whole Murther, reading the same to *Lewson*. Upon
which Mr. *Prance* ask'd him who gave him all that exact Account? He answered, *Girald* gave it him to shew it to the Lord
Bellasis, and the rest concerned.

17. Then away they went together all Three to *Bow* to a
Tavern, being the *Queens-Head*, one Mr. *Cashes* House, where
they went up one pair of Stairs, and there Mr. *Vernatti* wrote a
Note to one Mr. *Dethwick* who lived about a mile and an half
off, (as Mr. *Prance* thinks, about *Poplar*) to come to him, and
causes a Messenger to be provided to carry it, who was a Cobler,
whom he strictly charged not to deliver the same to any but
Dethwick's own hand, and if he were not at home to bring it
back again; whilst he was gone, looking out at the Window,
and hearing Fish cried, Mr. *Prance* bought some, and ordered
the people of the House to dress them. But after some time, both
Vernatti and *Lewson* went down to desire the Woman not to fry
them with Suet but with Butter; saying they would allow her
so much the more for dressing, pretending fat would rise in their
Stomachs; but the true reason which they declared above, was
because it was Fryday (being as he remembers the Friday next
after the Proclamation came forth, commanding Papists to depart
the City.) Thus nice and scrupulous were they in that paltry
Ob-

Obfervation, who could abett, counfel, and without the leaft remorfe, carry on a moft Hellifh Plot, and premeditated Murther. Yet was not this Caution fo neatly delivered, but that the people began to have a fufpicion that they were *Papifts*; for having a Barrel of *Colchefter* Oyfters brought, the Cobler return'd with word, That Mr. *Dethwick* would prefently be there; who came accordingly, and was entertain'd by *Vernatti* with abundance of Complaifance and Careffes; fo fell to their Oyfters, and preparing for Dinner: Mr. *Vernatti* was fo eager to communicate the bufinefs, that he had got the before-mentioned Narrative of Sir *Edmundbury's* Death in his hand, and was reading the fame to *Dethwick*, who faid the fame was very well; but a Boy of the Houfe obferving a paper in his hand, and having fome fufpicion, becaufe he heard the name of Sir *Edmundbury Godfrey* mentioned (as he hath fince made Oath) did liften at the door, till Mr. *Prance* perceiving fomething ftir behind the door, and being (as the Guilty always are) full of fufpicions and jealoufies, ran to the door, and opening it, found him there, and threatned to kick him down Stairs; and from that time they would not fuffer the door any more to be fhut, becaufe no body fhould liften. However there they continued all that day, and at night went every one to his home.

18. Soon after this, *Vernatti* was very importunate with Mr. *Prance* to go out of Town with him; whether it were to have done him a mifchief, as fearing to put confidence in him, and fufpecting he fhould difcover them, he knows not, but abfolutely refufed to go with him. This *Vernatti* is a perfon that has been a great Traveller, and liv'd a long time at *Rome*, maintaining a Correfpondence both in *France* and *Italy* with Jefuits and other the moft dangerous Popifh Firebrands; he frequently made it his bufinefs to carry away young Gentlemen to *Rhemes*, *Doway*, and other Foreign Seminaries, and fometimes young Ladies to Nunneries. In a word, he was a mighty ftickler in the Catholick Caufe, and a perfon fo dangerous, that 'tis pity he has efcaped the hand of Juftice.

19. Thus far this Execrable Murther was carried on in fecret, and the parties concern'd began to be out of all pain concerning it, not dreading any difcovery; but at laft the righteous God by an unexpected means was pleafed to lay open the fame, and in infinite mercy to bring Mr. *Prance* (whom the vile Priefts perfwafions, as aforefaid, had drawn in to be an Accomplice, and hardned fo far as not to have any due fenfe of the Guilt he had

con-

contracted) to be deeply affected with the horror of that crime, heartily penitent for the fame, and inftrumental towards a full difcovery The bringing this to pafs was moft affuredly the over-ruling hand of a fpecial Providence, as appears by the ftrange-nefs of the Circumftances which contributed to his being firft queftion'd for the fame.

For the better underftanding whereof, we muft acquaint the World with an Accident that happened before the Murther com-mitted, which yet cafually occafion'd it's difcovery fo long after.

Upon the firft notice of the Plot and Commitment of *Fen-wick, Ireland*, and the reft of the Traitors that were firft ap-prehended, Mr. *Prance* being then blindly zealous for Popery, happening to be in a Coffee-houfe where fome people were talking of the faid Prifoners, for the credit of the Catholick caufe did there fpeak words in their favour, which fome of the Com-pany thought *ill*, and gave (as he was told) fome information againft him ; whereof having notice, to avoid trouble and charge, he did abfent himfelf from his Houfe the three Nights next, and immediately after *Michaelmas* day , *viz.* on the Monday and Tuefday nights he lay at a Friends Houfe right over againft his Dwelling ; and on Wednefday-night at an Houfe by the *Mews-gate*. But then underftanding that the bufinefs was over, and no profecution like to be made on it, he afterwards lay at home as before, and this was very near a Fortnight before Sir *Edmund-bury* was murther'd. Yet by occafion of this, twelve weeks after Mr. *Prance* was call'd in queftion ; for there happening fome mif-underftanding between a Neighbour and him, who having got fome Intelligence that he once lay three Nights out of his Houfe, he will not fay out of ill will, becaufe he acknowledges the hand of God in it, but upon a miftake it was that he did imagine, that thefe might be the Nights whereon Sir *Edmundbury Godfrey* was murthered, and thofe that fucceeded it ; and upon this naked fur-mife, bottom'd upon nothing that he or any that he could pro-duce (though Mr. *Prance's* Servants were fcrutiniz'd) knew of the matter, a Warrant was obtain'd from the moft Honourable Council-Board to apprehend and examine Mr. *Prance* touching that matter. Being taken upon that Warrant on the 21 of *Dec.* laft being St. *Thomas* his day, he was firft carried into the Lobby by the Houfe of Commons, where Mr. *Bedlow* whom he did not know, having but once been feen by him before, *viz.* between the Murther and carrying out of the Body of Sir *Edmundbury Godfrey*

Godfrey, and at a time when Mr. *Prance* did not obferve him, yet knew his face again, and charg'd him pofitively with being concern'd in that Murther, and thereupon after Examination he was committed to *Newgate* on Saturday the 21 of *December*.

Upon the Monday following he made a Difcovery upon Oath, and then did Impeach the faid *Fitz-Girald*, *Dominick Kelly*, *Robert Green*, *Henry Berry*, and *Laurence Hill*; of thefe the two fubtle Priefts made fhift to efcape; *Girald* having not fince been heard of, but *Kelly* was got into the Prifon of the *Marfhalfeys* by the name of *Daniel Edmonds*, being taken up fomewhere in the County of *Surrey* where he retired to hide himfelf, and fent thither for being a Recufant; and hearing of *Prance's* being apprehended, made all the Intereft he could to be gone, and fo procured unknown Bail hired for 10 s. a piece, and got away in *December*, before he was known to be *Kelly*; though fince there hath been a full Difcovery thereof made publick; as for *Hill* and *Berry* they were forthwith taken at their own Houfes, but *Green* was before clapt up a Prifoner in the Gatehoufe for refufing to take the Oath, (for his Confcience was wonderful tender in that, but able to digeft a Murther.) And when his Keeper came to acquaint him that there was another Bufinefs come againft him, and that he was charg'd with the Murther of Sir *Edmundbury Godfrey*, he haftily askt, Who accufed him? and the Keeper telling him, It was one *Prance*: he prefently clapt his hand on his Breaft, and faid thefe words, *Then am I a dead man*.

20. On the 24th of *December*, *Prance* was carried before the King and Council, where he gave a particular account of the Circumftances of the Murther, as herein before is fet forth; and for more full fatisfaction touching the feveral places he had had occafion to mention, his Majefty thought fit to appoint his Grace the Duke of *Monmouth*, the Right Honourable the Earl of *Offory*, the Earl of *Clarendon*, and Sir *Robert Southwell*, Clerk of the Council, to go with him and take his Examination on the place, and fee if he could fhew all the particular places he had mentioned to the Board: Being come there he fhew'd his Grace, and thofe Noble Lords, firft, the fatal fpot, or place where Sir *Edmundbury Godfrey* was murthered, the place where *Berry* was affigned to ftand, and where himfelf ftood; then the door he was carried in at by the end of the Stables, the Stairs, the long dark Entry, the door leading to Doctor *Godwin's* Lodgings, the little Chamber there where the Body was firft laid; going to them all as readily as a man could do to any room in his own Houfe, which all appeared to be exactly fituate as he had defcribed them that morning before to the

G

Board.

Board. But as to that Room where he saw the Body lie on the Monday-night, being cross the upper Court, (though he carried them directly towards the place cross the Court, and told His Grace so far he was sure he was right, yet there being several Rooms, and he having never been there but once, and that in the night, and only with a dark Lanthorn,) he was not able certainly to assign the very Room. But as to all the other places he was positive, and so his Grace and their Honours return'd very well satisfied in the reality of his Information.

21. Here is to be noted, That whilst they were viewing Doctor *Godwin's* Lodgings, *Mrs. Broadstreet*, the Doctor's House-keeper, coming to understand what it was for, and that *Hill* their Servant was charged with the murther of Sir *Edmundbury Godfrey*, she (like a right Papist, to keep up the reputation of the party) voluntarily offered her Oath, and did swear before the Duke of *Monmouth*, That the said *Hill* had taken an House in *Stanhop*-street, and went thither to live and lodge at *Michaelmas*; whereas in truth, and at the Tryal of the said *Hill*, &c. it was plainly made appear before her face, That the said *Hill* did not go to reside at such his new house so soon, but continued his Lodging here till about three Weeks after *Michaelmas*, in which time all these Transactions concerning the murther, happened. She then further swore, That there was but one Key belonging to the outward door of their Lodgings, and so it was impossible that *Hill* should go out and in, and all these things be done, and they within not see him, or take notice of them: and yet before they went away from thence, Mr. *Prance* made it appear, and she was forc'd to confess, That there were four or five Keys amongst them thereunto, one of which *Hill* did always use to carry about him, that he might at any time come in, and go out at his pleasure without troubling or disturbing the rest of the Family; and Mr. *Prance* himself hath been several times let in by him therewith, they in the inner rooms taking no notice, as he could perceive.

22. But now because Mr. *Prance* would conceal nothing, but impartially set forth all that happened in this matter, he must not omit the Relation of that imbecillity (or what else sober and unbiass'd Judges shall please to call it) which has been so much talkt of, and variously reported.

Most true it is, though the sense of the bloody crime that he had been concern'd in, did (in spight of all the Popish Doctrines he had imbib'd) work such Convictions now on Mr. *Prance* his awakened Conscience, as to make this real Confession; yet by the horror there-

of,

of, the danger his life was in, the apparent hazard of being utterly
undone, together with a certain respect which he still bore towards
that Religion he had been bred in, and other selfish Considerati,
ons, he was once, for avoiding (as he then conceived) these dangers,
betray'd by humane frailty so far to retract by word of mouth
what he had before most truly confessed upon Oath, as to say before the King and Council, *That he was innocent, and they all* (meaning the rest accused) *were innocent*; and that was the substance of all
he then and there declared in that kind; For which he humbly
begs pardon of God, His Majesty, and that Honourable Board, and
the World. And though he dare not go about to excuse the same
wholly, yet there are several Circumstances that much alleviate
it, and render it insignificant to invalidate what he had before truly
set forth. For,

1. What he before declared concerning the Murther in manner
before herein set forth, was solemnly upon Oath; this supposed
Retractation was suddenly done under consternation and fear, and
not upon Oath.

2. He was at that time under certain danger of his life if he
persisted in that Confession, for he had no pardon granted, nor any
certainty of obtaining the same.

3. If he should obtain his pardon, he considered, That yet his
Life would be still in danger from the revengeful and bloody Priests
and Jesuits.

4. His mind was sorely troubled, as with all these dangers, so with
this further apprehension, That if he should escape with his Life,
yet by this discovery he should lose his Livelihood, and in all humane probability both he and all his Family be utterly undone; for
as he was the Queens Servant, and that his Trade and subsistence
chiefly, or indeed wholly depended on Her Majesties Custom,
(which was certain and considerable) and that of other Roman-
Catholicks; so it was not to be doubted but the most crafty and implacable Priests would soon use means by false Representations and
scandal, to deprive him thereof if he proceeded in this detection.

5. He retained still a certain respect to the Popish Religion in
which he had so long been educated; for he had not yet intirely
got his Soul out of that snare, and therefore he did then conceive,
being swayed by such powerful Inducements, That he might lawfully say, He was innocent, and so they were All; which in Popish construction is not to deny that they killed Sir *Edmundbury
Godfrey*, for that according to their Divinity, and what the said Priests
had solemnly declared, was no sin or crime, and consequently they
might

might all in such their Catholick sense still be *innocent* ; yet this he must acknowledge he somewhat doubted of, because he had never been at Confession, and received Absolution, since the Fact committed, which all the rest (as some of themselves had declar'd) had done, and so might more peremptorily persist (as they did) in averring themselves to be innocent ; and he does ingenuously declare, That had he received Absolution, 'tis his fear he should never, or not without extream difficulty have been brought to any acknowledgment.

These Circumstances, together with a great distemper of Body contracted by the incommodities of Confinement, want of Air, &c. occasion'd that sudden revolt of his reason and duty under that perplexity of spirit ; but as soon as he had done it, Conscience flew in his face, and would no longer be laid asleep with any delusive Popish Charms ; when he began to recollect himself, the power of Truth dispersed all these temptations of Interest, fear and superstition. If it were true, that he might hazard his Life and lose his Trade, if he did persist in the Confession of the Murther ; it was as true, and he found it by experience, that he should never have peace of Conscience if he denied it.

And therefore he was no sooner return'd from the King and Council to *Newgate* (which coming in a Coach 'tis certain was not half an hour) but he most earnestly requested Capt. *Richardson* (who had been with him, and heard what he had said that morning) for Gods sake to go back and assure the King and that Honourable Board from him, That the first Confession which he had made on Oath was true in all Circumstances ; and that whatsoever he had said before them that morning to the contrary, was occasion'd only by the consternation, fear, and perplexity of mind he was under, which the Captain immediately did, and hath since declared the same upon Oath.

23. The next day he grew more sick, insomuch that his life was despaired of, continuing so for about a week ; during this sickness, the Reverend Dr. *Lloyd*, Dean of *Bangor*, was charitably pleased to give him a Visit, & bestow'd much pains with him at several times, instructing him in the grounds and reasons of the Protestant Religion, from whose pious Admonitions & labours, by the Divine Blessing, he reaped much benefit for the comfort and setling of his perplexed Soul, and thinks it his duty for the same publickly to return him his hearty Thanks, being wholly taken off from the Apostatiz'd bloody Roman Church, which he utterly renounces, and doth freely, cordially, and intirely embrace the Protestant Religion, and therein particularly submits himself to the Church of *England*, resolving (by Gods Grace) therein to live and die.   After

24. After God had been pleased to restore in some measure his health, having given several Instances of stedfastness to his first Confession, by making some further Discoveries in the mean time, he was again carried before the King's most excellent Majesty and the Right Honourable the Lords of the Council, and there being largely re-examined, repeated his former Discoveries, agreeing in all Circumstances ; and then his Majesty was Graciously pleased with his own Royal Lips to give him assurance of his Gracious Pardon, and soon after the same was perfected in due Form of Law, under the Great Seal of *England*. For which with deepest sense of humility and gratitude, he declared himself ever ready to pay most hearty thanks in all observance and duty, desiring no longer to enjoy that life which he holds by his Royal Favour, than he shall upon all occasions imploy it to the utmost of his Capacity in his Majesties Service, for the Safety of his Sacred Life, the Welfare of his Kingdoms, and the Interest of the true Protestant Religion.

But whereas by Popish Adversaries there have been several false and scandalous Reports invented and spread abroad, that he was rackt or tortured in *Newgate*, and with harsh usages forced to confess what he did touching the Treasons and Murther aforesaid, he does declare the same are wholly false, and that on the contrary he did the same freely within two days after he was brought in there, and that he received several Civilities from Captain *Richardson*, during his Confinement under his Custody.

And he does protest in the presence of God, the searcher of hearts, before whose just and dreadful Tribunal we must all appear, that as to the whole Discovery and Evidence he hath given, he hath not therein been byassed with any malice or sinister ends, nor done any wrong to any of the persons accused ; but shall conclude this impartial Account of Sir *Edmundbury Godfrey*'s Murther, with his most hearty prayers, *That as he hath obtained the King's Majesty's Gracious Pardon here on Earth, for his heinous Crime in being so Accessary to the Death of that innocent worthy Gentleman ; so on sincere Repentance, and through the only merits of Jesus Christ, he may for the same receive forgiveness from the King of Kings in the World to come.*

The

The Popish Conspiracy to Murther the Right Honourable the Earl of Shaftsbury, and some other Contrivances after Sir Edmunbury Godfrey's Death.

AFter the Murther of Sir *Edmunbury Godfrey*, and some farther Discovery of the Plot, there was no person (next to his Sacred Majesty) against whom the malice of these Popish Conspirators was more directly levelled, than at the Right Honourable the Earl of *Shaftsbury*, as knowing that till so able a Statesman, and vigilant and active a Patriot, firm to the true Interest of his King and Country, and zealous for the preservation of the Protestant Religion, was taken out of the way, their cursed Machinations would be frustrated, and their wicked Designs be rendred ineffectual. And therefore they not only by their Emissaries and Abetters, both formerly and of late, had endeavoured to asperse his Honour, but also entred into a formal Conspiracy and Resolution to murther him, and engaged several barbarous Villains to do it ; though by the Providence of Heaven over his Noble Person, and a timely Discovery, happily prevented.

1. About five Weeks before *William Staley* (lately executed for Treason) was apprehended, Mr. *Prance* was with one Mr. *Messinger* (Gentleman of the Horse to the Lord *Arundel* of *Warder*, and formerly named in this Narrative for a Design to Murther his Sacred Majesty) one *Proffer* a Silver-smith, and one *Matteson* a Barber then living in *Holbourn*, all rank desperate Papists, at Mr. *Bradley's* an Alehouse in *Holbourn* ; where the said Mr. *Messinger* grievously complained of the severity of the Laws that were against the *Roman Catholicks*, expressing his apprehensions that they would now be rigorously put in Execution against them, by some that were not lovers of their party, and particularly he named the Earl of *Shaftsbury* as one of their most dangerous Enemies, and who did most concern himself about them, and in discovering the Plot, and therefore he said, There must be some effectual means used to rid him out of the world, and declared, that it was already resolved on.

2. That about a Fortnight, or near thereabouts, before the said *Staley's* Apprehension, he was in Company with the said *Staley*,

and

and the said *Matteson*, at the Cross-Keys Tavern over against Mr. *Staley's* Father's House, where in discourse they were complaining of the great Afflictions the Catholicks lay under, and what severe Usages they must further expect, if once this Plot should come to be believed, and be made out against them; and thereupon the said *Matteson* said, That if they did not take some speedy course to destroy some particular persons that were their most active Enemies, they (meaning the *Roman* Catholicks in general) should be ruined, and therefore in the first place (said he) we resolve to kill my Lord *Shaftsbury*, (whom he then called *The Ringleader of the mischief which they feared would fall upon them:*) And further, the said *Matteson* said, That he would engage three more to assist in that work of killing the said Earl, whose Names he then and there declared; that is to say, one *Adamson* a Watch-maker, and the said *Prosser*, and one *Bradshaw* an Upholsterer.

3. That some short time after the said *Matteson* came to Mr. *Prance's* Shop, and pulled a Pistol out of his Pocket, saying, *This shall do Shaftsbury's business*; declaring he had provided the same on purpose for killing the said Earl.

4. That afterwards Mr. *Prance* met with the beforenamed *Adamson* at Mr. *Pedley's* at the White Posts in *Vere-street*; where discoursing of News, *Adamson* said, That the Catholicks would be all undone, if they did not look about them, and therefore they were resolved to kill the Lord *Shaftsbury*: against whom, upon all occasions or mention, both he and the other Persons before nominated, expressed the utmost malice and hatred imaginable, as being, they said, most likely to obstruct and frustrate their Designs: Likewise the said *Adamson* another time, not long after, did again express such Design to murther the said Lord, and then owned that he himself in particular was engaged therein, and would kill him as soon as he could get an opportunity: which words were by him uttered at the Sign of the Gridiron, an Alehouse in *Holborn*.

5. About the same time the before-named *Prosser* coming to Mr. *Prance's* Shop, did likewise tell him, That he did resolve to kill the Lord *Shaftsbury*, and assigned this reason or provocation which incited him thereunto, *viz. For that he the said Earl of* Shaftsbury *and some other Protestant Lords, did intend to ruine the Lord* Arundel *of* Warder, *on the account of the Plot, which Lord* Arundel (as he said) *was his the said Prosser's very good Customer and Benefactor.* And also the said *Prosser* did, at Mr. *Bradley's* House in *Holborn*, declare, that he was to be an Ensign under the said Lord *Arundel* in the

Forces

Forces which were to have been raised by the Conspirators, for the Subversion of the Government, and Extirpation of the Protestant Religion.

6. That the beforenamed *Bradshaw*, about the same time, *viz.* the first or second Week of *November*, came to Mr. *Prance*'s Shop one day, and in discourse did say, That he would make no more to kill a Protestant than to kill a Dog or a Cat, which he pronounced with a great deal of vehemency and earnestness, and said moreover, That he was resolved to dispatch some of those busie Heretical Lords, but the first should be the Lord *Shaftsbury* : and likewise the said *Bradshaw* pulled out a Pistol, and shewed the same in the said Shop, declaring that he had prepared the same to do the said Execution therewith.

7. That the said *Bradshaw* is a violent cruel Papist, of most dangerous Principles, and fit to be employed in such assassinating bloody Attempts, appears by this Instance, That about three years ago being with some Company in a Shop in *Dukes-street*, discoursing, and seeing a little Child passing by, he voluntarily said, that he would make no more to kill that heretical Child than to kill a Dog.

8. That another time the before-named *Prosser*, at Mr. *Bradley*'s House in *Holbourn*, did declare, That the before-mentioned Mr. *Messinger* (Gentleman of the Horse to the Lord *Arundel* of *Warder*) was the person that principally promoted the killing of the Lord *Shaftsbury*, and that he himself was engaged therein, and did not doubt but in short time to get an opportunity to effect the same.

9. That Mr. *Henry Nevil* is very intimate with the before-mentioned *Prosser*, and hath for a long time been aiding and assisting to him, and doth hold a Correspondence with the Lords in the Tower, and with some persons at *Rome*, sending Letters duly thither, and receiving great Pacquets back again from thence very frequently ; and that one of his Servants having several of the said Letters in his Trunk, the said Mr. *Nevil* about   last caused the said Trunk to be broke open (the Fellow being then in the Country) and took away the said Papers, to prevent any Discovery that might be made thereby.

10. That Mr. *Richard Nevil*, Nephew to the said *Henry Nevil*, did maintain a Correspondence with the Lords in the Tower in a very suspicious manner, *viz.* Dressing himself in a Coach-mans Habit, he drove his own Coach, wherein rode his Coachman in the Equipage of a Gentleman, and taking upon him the Name

of

of Squire *Duck* ; who being come to the Tower, this pretended Squire *Duck* commanded the disguised Coach-man (who was his real Master) to go in to the Lords, and present his most Humble Service to them, and to tell them, that he came as nigh them as he could, and should be most glad to hear of their good healths ; in which disguise the said *Nevil* went up to their Lordships Lodging, and stayed with them a considerable time, whilst the true Coachman remained in the Coach. But soon afterwards the said *Duck* was removed from that Imploy of Coach-man, and sent away into the Country ; for fear, as is most probable, that he should discover this and other the like Actions of the said two Gentlemen ; this Relation came from the said Coach-mans own Mouth.

11. That in the Month of *October* last Mr. *Prance* met with one Mr. *Cozeen*, a *French* Papist, and by Trade a Taylor, who walking together in *Covent-Garden*, and discoursing of News ; The said *Cozeen* said, that the King and Parliament designed to undo us, (meaning the *Romanists*,) But, said he, if I were to kill a man, I would kill the King as soon as any man, and if we had him in *France* we would have killed him before now ; intending thereby, as he understood him, and as the Natural Sense of that Expression imports, to magnifie the Courage and Zeal of their *French* Papists, and how ready they would be to kill their King, if he were of another Religion, which he proposed as an Example that he would have English *Roman* Catholicks to imitate ; and another time, not long after, the said *Cozeen* spake the same words, or to the very same effect in *Prance*'s Shop.

I   A BRIEF

A BRIEF

DETECTION

OF THE

Immoral Behaviour, Cruel Expressions, and Vile Practi-
ses of several other Popish Priests with whom M. P.
hath been acquainted.

Aving thus faithfully and impartially made a candid
Discovery of the several Traiterous and Bloody Intrigues carried on by the Papists, herein before set forth,
we shall thereunto add a short Account of the Man-
ners of divers *Romish* Priests, with whom Mr. *Prance* hath had
Conversation; which he does protest to do, not out of any malice
to their Persons, but out of detestation to their dangerous Principles and lewd Practises, and more especially that others whom
Education or crafty Insinuations have brought up in, or inveigled
to the *Romish* Communion, may reflect and consider what kind
of people they are whom they blindly follow, and thereby be a-
wakened to forsake such wicked and beastly Guides, and no longer be led astray by them, to the dishonour of God, scandal of
Christian Religion which they pretend to profess, disturbance of
Government, danger of their Neighbours, and hazard of their
own souls.

1. Amongst

1. Amongst many other Priests he had a particular acquaintance with one Mr. *Matthews*, that was Priest to the Lord *Peters*, who was a very bitter Enemy to all Protestants, and hath several times said, *That they* (meaning the Protestants) *were all certainly and infallibly damn'd, and that it was impossible for a Soul of them to be saved*; further adding, *that to kill any of them was no Sin, especially if it were for the Interest of the Church*; and the like wicked and cruel Expressions: He also in or about the Month of *August* last, said, That his Lord and the Lord *Bellasis*, with some other Catholick Lords, would e're long have a good Army on foot, and that all the Devils in Hell could not prevent it, but the Catholick Religion would quickly be settled in *England*. We may believe him, that the Devils would not prevent or hinder it, since it was so much their Interest to have it establish'd, especially by such bloody and hellish means as the Conspirators were resolved to make use of for that purpose; but God has hitherto, and we hope will still be Graciously pleased to prevent their Designs. This Gentleman was a great Dealer in Reliques and *Agnus Dei's*, and hath cheated divers ignorant devout people (as hath been credibly reported) of considerable Sums of Money for such Trumpery. He hath oftentimes, with much reverence and ceremony, as kissing them, *&c.* shewed Mr. *Prance* several pieces of Bones, which he said were the Bones of such and such He-and-She Saints, whose Names he had at his Tongues end, and attributed most wonderful Vertues to them; for he hath affirmed, That they being worn about one, would keep the Devil from one, so that not only he should have no power to hurt ones Person, but not so much as to tempt those to sin that carried them about them: That in a Tempest they would preserve one from drowning, and if an House were on Fire, if you cast in one of them, the same would presently stop the Fire, *&c.* But as to the last it is apparent, that he and his Brethren, the Popish Priests and *Jesuits*, are far more dexterous Artists in contriving Devices to burn down Houses, than to quench them when on Fire.

2. There was occasion before to mention one *Singleton* a Priest, that declared, *He would make no more to stab forty Parliament Men, than to eat his Dinner*; besides his Quality of Priest, he was also a kind of Sollicitor or Broker amongst the Papists, making it

his

his Business to get other Peoples Money into his Hands, and put it out to Use; in which Traid he plaid the Extortioner most egregiously, for all that he could get above the due Interest of six pounds *per Cent.* being to be put in his own Pocket, he would not let forty or fifty pounds out for six Months, but he would have forty Shillings for Procuration, which must be deducted on the first issuing of the Money, and yet the full Legal Interest to run on; and besides he always would fill up the Bond himself; and for that Business, (for which no Scrivener ever asked above twelve pence,) he would make the poor people pay five Shillings: These Practises of his Mr. *Prance* can affirm on his own knowledge; and there are divers who have dealt with him on these terms who can testifie the same; and yet this Ghostly Father was a great Preacher against Covetousness and Usury; but it seems he meant only in others, not himself: For in other Cases likewise he allowed himself the like Priviledges, for he would frequently be Drunk, and stay out till one or two of the Clock in the Morning, or after, and yet go the same Forenoon to say Mass, and consequently received the Sacrament, which they teach the People must in no wise be done, unless the Party be strictly fasting.

3. Mr. *Byfleet* and Doctor *Guilding*, two Priests, have severally declared in Mr. *Hall* the Cook's House, and divers other places, That they respectively had turned several People from the Protestant Religion, and reconciled them to the Church of *Rome*, in the City of *London*, and that they hoped they should turn many more. They were both Persons of a very vicious Conversation, but slily carried it. *Byfleet* was a mighty Magnifier of the Vertues and Necessity of Fasting to other People in *Lent, Ember-days, &c.* but as for himself, could frequently, as is well known, dispense with six Penny-worth of Victuals, and a Quart or two of Ale, all alone for a Breakfast or Supper on the same days in his Chamber. As for Doctor *Guilding*, he was his Cousin, and (they said) had read Philosophy many years at *Doway*, but very much forgot his Ethicks in *England*, being so filthily addicted to lewd Women, that one could not but conclude he received his Ordination from Pope *Joan*, or some of her fulsom Successors.

These

These two last named, and *Singleton*, were most frequently at Mr. *Hall* the Cook's House in *Ivy Lane*, and there they dined, and Mr. *Prance* does verily believe, that those many *Popish* Books being above a Cart-load and an half, with the *Priests* Vestments, Beads, Images, and other superstitious Trumpery, which were lately found there in searching of his House, did belong to them; And the said *Hall* (as he likewise believes) does know where they are, or were, since they absconded themselves: for which suspicion there are these two grounds. First, Because whenever about *November* or *December* last, he came to speak with *Singleton* or either of the others; he the said *Hall* undertook to take his business, and must needs deliver it to *Singleton*, because when he called again he failed not to give M. *P.* an Account of it from him; Secondly, Because Mr. *Hadden* Servant to Doctor *Parrot*, the Superior of Secular *Priests*, told him, That always when he came with money to be distributed for Masses for the dead, *Hall* took the money that was designed for *Singleton*, and conveyed it to him. The meaning of which is thus, When any Roman *Catholick* dies, 'tis probable there is a Priest (sometimes two or three) by him, who never fail to put him in mind, and frighten him with the pains of Purgatory, and of the Virtues of Masses said to ease and deliver them from the same so much the sooner, so that being therewith terrified, if he be a Person of any considerable Quality or Estate, it seldom happens but he leaves so much money to pray his Soul out of Purgatory, then this money is paid in to the Superior, who thereupon according to the Sum, sends to so many Priests so many Shillings a piece, for which they are each to say so many Masses for the deceased; the Common price of Mumbling over a Mass being accounted 12 *d.* And as for this Doctor *Parrot*, who is, or lately was the Head of all this sort of *Priests* in *England*, 'tis very credibly informed, That he hath been seen in Bed with a Whore, by the said Mr. *Hadden* his Servant, who told the same to Mr. *Prance*.

4. But as whoring is counted but a Venial Sin by *Papists* in general; so amongst them scarce any are more devoted thereunto than their Ghostly Fathers, who rail so loud at the *Protestant Clergy* for having honest Wives of their own. About three years ago one *Kelly* an *Irish* Priest, (a Kinsman to the before named *Dominick Kelly*, concern'd in the Murther of Sir *Edmundbury Godfrey*) being just arrived from *France* or *Flanders*, was brought to lodge at Mr. *Prance's* House, and the very first Night, the maid going up with him to warm his Bed, he began to use some Incivilities, which

K   she

she modestly opposing, he proceeded to use violence, and would
have Ravisht her, insomuch that she cryed out, and Mr. Prance's
Wife hastning up Stairs, and perceiving his rudeness, being af-
frighted run down again, fearing he would have done her some
mischief, and called in some Neighbours, who immediately coming in, caused him to desist: for which M. P. Wife would presently
have turn'd him out of doors, but it being late in the Night, and
he wholly a Stranger in the Town; He would not (though he
were a Rogue) be so inhospitable to him; but suffered him to
stay till morning; However they were obliged to burn Candle all
Night for fear in Revenge he should do them a mischief.

5. One *Dowdal* being Colonel *Talbot's* Priest at *Twitnam*, some
few years ago, and under that Quality much Entrusted, stole
and run away with the Chalice, Crewet, Bason, Rich Copes, Ve-
stiments, Surplices and other Sacred Gear, provided for him to officiate the Mass with, and being wholly a Stranger, exposed the
Bason and Crewet to Sale at Mr. *Prance's* Shop, who fairly and at
at a valuable price bought the same. The Priest having received
his money, invited him into a Tavern, and afterwards agreed, That
he should come next day to his Lodging in *White-Fryers*, and see
the Vestments, Linnen and other things; which he did and offered
him 8 *l.* but he would not take under 12 or 15 *l.* However he
would go again to drink, and at last walkt with Mr. *Prance* home,
who leaving him in a Parlour, where there was a little Girl of a-
bout 6 years of Age, whil'st he went to attend some Customers
in the Shop, this Goatish Priest began to play the Villain with the
Child, and would have spoil'd her, (had she not cry'd out) with
his impudent Rudeness, which made him run in to see what was
the matter, and occasioned the other to hasten away, and presently
shifted his Lodging: for going next day to look after him he was
gone, out of fear (as is supposed) of being apprehended for the
Robbery; of which yet there was no great danger; For though
within a day or two Mr. *Prance* heard of the Robbery, by one that
was a Servant to the Colonel, yet such was the said Colonel's extreme Zeal, and so prevalent above the Resentment of his loss,
that (as he was by that Servant assured) as soon as he discovered
what their Priest had done, he called all his People together, and
did solemnly charge them not to speak thereof to any Person, because if known, it would be a foul scandal to their Religion: Adding, that if he found any of them should utter a word of it he
would

would run them through ; A Seal of Secresie, (when ones life lies at Stake) almost as firm as that of Confession.

About 4 years ago there was one Mr. *Thomas Sheepherd*, a person related to Mr. *Prance*, who being Sick, sent to him to procure a *Romish* Priest to come to him, Mr. *Prance* much wondered at his desire, as having always accounted him a Protestant, however it being his Request, and understanding he was very ill, and not likely to Live, he did endeavour to get one. And thereupon repaired to Doctor *Hanson* a Carmelite, at *Wild House*, one of their Superiors, who directed him to Doctor *Clement Mutus*, a Benedictin Monk belonging to the *Spanish* Ambassador, but lodging then at one *Ireland*'s a Tobaconist in *Verestreet*. Having told him the Story, and what a work of Charity it would be to save a Soul, he readily condescended to go, and did give the man what advice he thought fit, *&c.* But the Sick party being very Poor did not give him any money, which as appears he expected ; for next day the man growing still weaker, sent to desire the same Priest again, to which purpose Mr. *Prance* went to request his Company. But here truly found the old Proverb verified, *No Penny, no Pater-Noster*, for this charitable Father told him, No, he would not, for he gave him nothing yesterday. Mr. *Prance* urged, that so good a Work as to reduce a dying Heretick to the Church would reward it self, and be meritorious. He replyed, he loved a Reward in hand, for all that of the other World ; *For* (said he) *they get Heaven by us, and why should not we get money by them :* The other insisted, that the man was very Poor, and had it not, and that he hoped he would not suffer his Soul to be lost ; Let his Soul, quoth he, do as it will, I am resolved not to go to any twice that do not pay me ; And so by no Intreaties could be induced to stir ; but the poor man soon after died. So sordidly covetous are these People. And notwithstanding all their pretences, have really so little Regard to the Salvation of men, that they would suffer a Soul to perish Eternally (as they say all do that die out of their Church's Communion) unless they can get money, by saving it, if indeed (as they impudently pretend) it lay in their power

There is another Priest that did likewise pretend to belong to the *Spanish* Ambassador, his name is *Collins*, who, 'tis said, is now in Custody, When his Majesties Proclamation came out some years ago, commanding away all Priests (but such as were allowed) And that none of his Subjects should go to hear Mass, this zealous Father got up on the Leads of *Sommerset-House*, and there held his Conventicle,

venticle, and faid Mafs, having a great Concourfe of People that followed him; yet this precious Saint, when a young Wench has come to him to Confeffion, hath been feen to get her between his Legs, and fo clofely hug, and kifs her many times over, as if it had been part of her Pennance to be moft filthily fnuggled. He was a common frequenter of Bawdy-Houfes, and has been obferved many times to come drunk out of fuch lewd places, in fuch filthy poftures, as 'tis a fhame here to relate.

There is alfo one *Davenport* a Friar, but of what Order, Mr. *Prance* does not remember, who calls himfelf, and is ufually ftyled, Captain *Davenport*. He is a kind of ftrowling, wandring Prieft that rides up and down the Countreys, but efpecially *Norfolk*, *Suffolk*, *Cambridgfhire* Ifle of *Ely*, &c. where he does abundance of mifchief in feducing people both from the Proteftant Religion, and their Allegiance to their Soveraign : For he makes it his whole Bufinefs to infinuate, carry News, unfettle weak Heads, abufe the Church of *England* and its Minifters and Afferters, magnifying the Holinefs, Piety, Charity, &c. of *Rome*, and by fuch his Arts perverting the minds of many ; For he has long followed this mifchievous Practice, never conftant in any place, but always in motion from one Gentleman's Houfe to another, and fometimes amongft people of mean Condition, to fpread his poifon the further ; As if he defign'd to infect the whole Country. He is no doubt a very dangerous Fellow, and no longer ago than the laft Summer was Twelve-month, there being a Chapter, (as they call it, that is, a General Convention) of Friars held in *Somerfet-Houfe*, whither many reforted both from beyond the Seas, and all Parts of this Realm ; On what Defign (whether to carry on the Great Work) Mr. *Prance* knows not, but hath fome reafon to fufpect it was for no good purpofe : For feeing about Twenty of them together, amongft the reft there was this Captain *Davenport*, whom he then heard fay, *That he hoped to be a Captain once again in the Catholick Caufe, before he died.*

There is one *Bully*, a Secular Prieft, who formerly did belong to a *French* Ambaffador, but of late his Trade has been to run about Hackneying forth of Maffes for Twelve-pence a piece at private Houfes, where ever he can get Cuftomers. He was mighty ftrict in his teaching (as they all do ;) That people muft by no means Eat or Drink a drop that morning on which they intend to Receive

ceive the Eucharift, before they come to Mafs, becaufe they muft receive ftrictly Fafting; Yet hath not only been frequently feen in his road to Mr. *Pafton's* in *Duke-Street* call in at an Ale-houfe, and take his Pot or more of Ale, and fo away to Mafs; (Now a Prieft cannot fay Mafs, but he himfelf muft needs receive.) But alfo he has been known at play at Cards, Tippling in Company, and Drunk after One a Clock in the Morning at *Pedley's* at the *White Pofts*, and yet the fame day Trudge to Mafs and earn a Shilling to furnifh a frefh Debauch. But thefe are not all the rare Qualities he has, For he is a notable Whore-monger too; Nay, (if the General Report be true that is Corrant amongft Catholicks) keeps another man's Wife; which *M. P.* is the rather inclined to believe, becaufe he hath often met them hand in hand in *Cheapfide*, and other places.

There is one *Holt* a Secular Prieft, that ufed to Officiate at the Lady *Sommerfets* in *Lincolns-Inn-Fields*, who is a virulent Enemy to all Proteftants, and hath often been heard by *M. Prance* to declare, That 'tis impoffible any of them fhould ever be faved. Now how ready a way this is to inflame Papifts againft them, and how apt will they be to cut their Throats, and any way deftroy thofe whom they are already made to believe are Enemies of God, and nothing but fit Fewel for Hell. And that this was his Defign, is moft probable both by the violent eagernefs of fuch his Expreffions, As alfo becaufe *M. Prance* hath often heard him fay, That he did not doubt but to fee Herefie rooted out, and the Catholick Religion e're long Eftablifht in *England*.

Father *James* an eminent Friar at *Somerfet-Houfe* lately deceafed, was for feveral years Confeffor to *M. Prance*, fo that he had with him an intimate Familiarity; About a year and a half ago difcourfing with him, He told him, That there would fhortly be on foot a Confiderable Force to fettle the *Roman* Catholick Religion in *England*; And that he did not Queftion but to fee it Eftablifh'd very fhortly. Upon which *M. Prance* faid to him, That he was confident that could never be done without oppofing his Majefty's Authority; and it would be a great fhame and fcandal to *Roman* Catholicks, who had valued themfelves fo much upon their Loyalty in the late Times, if they now fhould be Guilty of Rebellion againft their King. Whereunto he replyed, That in the Caufe of God there was no Confideration to be had of Princes;

L   That

That it was no Sin to be Active to suppress Heresie, and establish the Catholick Doctrine: For though Obedience was a Duty in other Circumstances, yet in this Case the Obedience to the Church was to be preferr'd; For the Civil Magistrates must submit to the Spiritual, and might lawfully be resisted, and That it was the duty of every Priest to give any man Absolution that should be concerned therein, with several other Seditious and Traiterous Expressions. And further M. Prance having at several times fallen into discourse upon some occasions concerning the nature of the Absolution given by him and other Priests, he the said Father James did declare, That such Absolution was a full and perfect Remission of Sin, and such an Acquittal as rendred any man as Innocent and free from Guilt as the first day he was born, from any actual Transgression. Then he ask'd him, for Example. If a person should commit a Sin, and confess it to him, or any other Priest, and receive an Absolution, and were afterwards taxed or questioned for that Fact Whether he might with a *safe Conscience, and without Sin say he was Innocent.* To which the said Father James replyed, That if such person had received such Absolution, and performed the Pennance imposed upon him, he may lawfully say, He was Innocent: for says he, When God by the mouth of his Priest, has absolved any Person, he becomes Innocent in the sight of God, and being so, has no Reason to impeach himself by owning of the Crime before men, nor cast a scandal on the Church, which to do would be a greater sin, than to deny a matter which he is no ways obliged to confess.

These and several other like Discourses to the same Purport and Effect hath the said Father James declared to M. Prance, inquiring his Instructions for the Direction of his Conscience; whereby may appear, by what measures such men steer the Soul of those that ignorantly commit themselves to their Conduct; and no wonder it will be, that some persons gasp out their last Breath with pronouncing a Lie, and persist to the utmost in denial of those Crimes, which both their own Consciences and the World know them to be guilty of, since they are before hand hardened into a Persuasion, That it is not Evil, but rather their Duty in respect to the Church's Interest so to do.

Jeremy Jennings, a Secular Priest, lately living at Mr. *Ramseys* near *Norwich* in *Norfolk,* a little after *Midsummer* last, both at Mrs. Halls

Halls in *Eagle-Court*, in the *Strand*, and in *M. Prance's* own Shop, told him, That we should shortly see better times, and that he did not doubt, but such Roman Catholick Priests as he was, should e're long walk publickly in Parsons Habits. He also hath reconciled several (as he hath acknowledged) to the Church of *Rome*, and amongst his Acquaintance was very free of his Beads, and Prayer-Books, and hath been heard to say Mass at Sir *Henry Bennifields*, at *Oxford-Hall* in *Norfolk*; So that by such his aforesaid Words, there is good reason to judge, that the said *Jennings* was acquainted with the Plot, nay, 'tis reasonable to believe, that there was not a Priest in *England*, nay, scarce any Gentleman of Note, or private Person of any Condition of the Roman Catholick Persuasion, but was privy unto the said Plot and Conspiracy, if not as to the particular Intrigues, yet at least as to the General Substance and Designs thereof.

There was one Monsieur *L. Hay* (to the best of *M. Prance's* remembrance, that was his right name) who not much above a year ago retaining to a Foreigner, a Person of Condition (whose Name and Quality is not convenient here to mention) did debauch a young Woman, and to avoid Charge that he suspected might ensue, by her proving with Child, procured a certain Person of his Acquaintance to be married unto her ; and after this, privately bargained to commit Adultery with her for so much a time ; which he practised so long without payment, that at last at the rate agreed on, he was Twenty Pounds in her debt, which refusing or avoiding to pay, the Woman impatient to be so served, did repair unto his Lord's House, and getting access to him, complain'd of his Priests owing her Twenty Pounds; who demanding for what ? She after some triflings of pretended Modesty, confest it was for the ill use of her Body ; the Gentleman surprised, and scarce believing her, ask'd her when the last time was that he had to do with her ? She answered on *Friday* last about Nine of the Clock in the Forenoon, the Gentleman remembring that his Priest was that day at Mass ; told her, She was certainly mistaken ; but she persevering in her Story, he call'd in the Priest, demanding if he owed her any Money, which he not being able to deny, nor yet to declare on what good account he became so indebted to her, his Master could not but conclude him Guilty, and began to upbraid him, saying, Are not you a most profane Villain to lye with this Woman at Nine a Clock and approach to the Altar, and offer to receive God's Body before Ten, and that without any Absolu-

tion

tion too? The Prieſt could not deny but that he was Rogue e-
nough, but as to the laſt Particular, aſſured him he had Abſoluti-
on. And being inquired how or from whom, after ſome Evaſions
he confeſt that another *French* Prieſt and he both lay with her ſuc-
ceſſively at that time, and that they mutually gave each other Ab-
ſolution; which is a notable Religious Method of whoring, and as
'tis likely often practiſed by theſe Ghoſtly Fathers. This Relation
M. Prance doth not aver upon his own knowledge, but knew the
ſaid *De la Hay* very well, and was moſt Credibly informed and
aſſured of the Truth thereof.

The foregoing Narrative touching the Murther of Sir *Edmundbury Godfrey*, and other Paſſages relating to the horrid *Popiſh* Plot,
were written by my Directions, and put into Method for the Preſs,
the matter being dictated by me, and taken all along from my
own Mouth. And having ſince peruſed it all over, I do own the
ſame, and atteſt the truth of the ſeveral particulars and things
therein contained, as they are there related and ſet forth.

Miles Prance.

F I N I S.